I Want to Go Home

AYRES GIPSON

PAGE PUBLISHING
Conneaut Lake, PA

First originally published by Page Publishing 2024

ISBN 979-8-89157-643-8 (pbk)
ISBN 979-8-89157-671-1 (digital)

Printed in the United States of America

To my son, grandchildren, and Mama.
Special thanks to Greta—you helped make this possible. Thank you.

KING STREET TRAIN STATION IS where I first arrived in Seattle. My immediate feeling was, I wanted to go home. Waiting patiently for my cousin to pick me up, I knew I came to Seattle to rehabilitate, a change in my life for the better and a release from drug addiction. I did not know that Seattle is infiltrated with illegal drugs; cocaine, heroin, and pills are everywhere. Sales on the streets were everywhere; it is a drug city. It only took me two weeks to learn this, but I'm here to rehabilitate, now.

I met this cousin at a family reunion in Louisiana. He has a business in trash hauling and owns an apartment building. He offered me a job and a place to live. I jumped at the chance, knowing nothing about Seattle but a chance to rehabilitate. You see, I have been doing illegal drugs since age fourteen. Another cousin introduced me to marijuana at that age. Then, at the age of twenty, my brother introduced me to cocaine. Around the time of my twenty-fifth birthday, I was not addicted yet. Powder cocaine was in my soul and brain. Although I was functioning normally; had a good job with IBM, a good home, and a car; and went on vacations, cocaine was becoming a big part of my life. Around age thirty-five, crack came into my life.

This is where my life story begins. I was born in 1953 to Fennis and Eddie Mary Gipson, named Ayres Andrea Gipson, at San Francisco General Hospital. I am American. Looking back and knowing what I know now, I was born in the spirit, feeling this at the age of five. Jim Crow was never legal in San Francisco, although it was practiced through real estate.

In my household growing up, there were two girls and two boys. Our father was previously married with children. At age five was when I first felt the spirit. We as a family would take a summer vacation yearly. Every two years, we would travel by car to Texas and Louisiana. Jim Crow was legal, even though it was not right. The color of someone's skin didn't have any effect on me, until meeting my father's cousin, who was married to a Caucasian woman. At the age of six or seven, after questioning the shit out of her and thinking it was great that she was married to a man of a different color, I felt unity. After that first meeting, they were some of my favorite people.

Cleophas and Ursula Brown were their names. The name Cleophas can be found in John 19:25, and he was a believer in God. I stayed in contact with them all the way until death do us part. I loved them very much. Feeling the spirit does not mean you know the spirit. I had this spirit in me not knowing how, what, or who it was. At this age, I did not know God. My mom had an influence over me, but I could not "see the forest for the trees."

What goes around, comes around. I shout that, yeah! The four major forms of worship, Christianity, Judaism, Islam, and Hinduism, all believe in what Buddha calls karma. You steal from someone, and then something will get stolen from you. You lie, and you'll be lied to. I did not learn this until age sixty. Oh, I know it well now. I'm conscious of it daily and loving this life.

As a kid, I wanted to be a cook. I remember my first recipe was pumpkin bread at age ten. My mother was amused by the bread saying, "He ate the whole thing." Since then, cooking has always been in my heart.

I played lots of sports growing up, around the age of thirteen, but was not very good. I was very uncoordinated physically. I played on several championship basketball teams, junior high and Woodrow Wilson high school. At Wilson, we went to the Bay Area Tournament of Champions and won. Prior to that, in junior high, we won the city championship. I was the best free-throw shooter. I also ran track. I was good at running. I am still a runner today. I had the spirit but no coordination. I learned to play tennis as an adult but was uncoordinated. I tried hard at tennis and played for more than fifteen years, still uncoordinated. I played in tournaments, trying to compete with the pros, but only living a dream. I was very happy to give the sport up. I didn't like the competition of someone losing or winning. With running, there is no competition, only self. I like that! Run, run, and run—I'm only competing with myself in trying to further my distance, stay agile, and coordinate. I had a very tragic accident in 1992, which I will talk about later. When running, the spirit is always with me. I love to run!

My first job came around 1967 at the age of fourteen, and the employer was my dad. I worked in the North Beach area of San Francisco, including Coit tower, Chinatown, and the Italian district. A lot of education for me came from North Beach. My dad did valet parking for a restaurant named Del Vecchios, located at that time on Broadway and Montgomery. He also parked for a nightclub named Andre's, which happens to be my middle name. He rented parking space from the old gay 90s club.

My first job was only to watch the cars with the keys inside them so that they would not be stolen.

I was sitting in a car when another one of my father's workers asked me, "Can you move the car back?"

I said, "Sure," knowing my dad had instructed me specifically not to move any cars. I did and backed up into another car, causing major damage. I just knew my dad was going to whip my ass, but the other worker took the blame for my mistake—whew, the spirit was definitely with me that night.

I thought making a career out of parking cars in North Beach was it! At the age of nineteen, I started my own valet service, parking for several restaurants and clubs. I had a parking lot, adjacent to an alley next to a Filipino restaurant. There I met Eddie Mesa (the Elvis Presley of the Philippines) and Ferdinand Marcos's brother who was said to be a doctor. During that time, the Philippines was under martial law, as they were trying to oust dictator Marcos.

I also parked for the On Broadway Theatre. I met actor Ben Vereen when he was working on the play *No Place to Be Somebody*. I also met Nick Stewart, the producer of *Norman…Is That You?* He played Lighting in the hit TV show *Amos and Andy*. He tried to get me into acting, but I was not interested. I parked cars for Basin Street West, an entertainment nightclub where a lot of famous rhythm and blues artists performed. These entertainers would perform there often, Ike and Tina Turner, The Delfonics, and Teddy Pendergrass. I learned a lot from seeing them perform. I played music in a band and would sometimes sing in harmony and lead, so seeing these entertainers was awesome.

One evening, a man approached me asking about the alley and parking lot, and I thought nothing of it. I learned he was interested in my business, and soon, I was out of business. Oh, this turned my life into a hellhole, married with a child and out of work with no career, but some college. I was the major financial provider of our family. North Beach was finished. My self-esteem and drive for success were gone. I did not know that the spirit was in me and only a small part of righteousness was in me, but God saved me. I then went out searching for a job and career. What was I going to do? As a student in high school, I worked a summer job at the San Francisco Naval Shipyard. I worked on the aircraft carrier Midway.

So let's take a look. Growing up, I was very insecure. I never felt good about myself, never, from age five until forty, insecurity. I know racial discrimination played a big part, but that was my problem. I didn't know how to deal with it, as a child or an adult. In 1992, I had an accident that caused a seven-day coma. After that coma for some strange reason, insecurity was greatly reduced. The coma was in 1992. So what was life for me from 1970 to 1992? Hell with a capital H. The spirit was within.

Valet parking ended in 1974 with me out of work. I began looking in the newspaper for job listings. I saw a listing for a sales representative, no experience necessary. I called and scheduled an interview. I met with an English man who was selling Royal Bond Copiers, dry copies. During this time, only wet copies were available, and the leading company was Savin. I got the job selling Royal Bond Copiers; they were very expensive, $10,000.00. I was first taught how to cold-call by phone or in person. This was work in unfamiliar territory, being African American and afraid of rejection, but persevering and feeling insecure, it was hard. I would cold-call in the mornings by phone and visit in person in the evening. Finally, over the phone, I got an appointment with a company in Palo Alto. I met with them and arranged for a demonstration at my office and sold it! They paid $10,000 for the copier, and my commission was $1,000.00. The spirit was with me, thank God. I wanted to celebrate. I arranged to cook breakfast for our company one Saturday morning, but no one showed up. My wife at this time was surprised. I was more embarrassed than hurt in front of her. The next week, I began to look for another job. I landed an interview with a 3M company, Minnesota Mining Manufacturing. They sold dry copiers too, and I got the job with a company car and expense account. I went through training in Carson in Southern California. The spirit was with me, again.

I could not forget and did not want to forget about North Beach and parking—it was in my heart. I had relatives who parked cars for the Playboy club. Across the street was an Arco station with a parking lot, and they were looking for an attendant. I applied and got the job on weekends. Bill Cosby was a regular in North Beach, both as a customer and a performer at several nightclubs. He also had a friend who worked at the Playboy club. I was dating his friend's sister. At this time, I was separated from my wife.

One night, Sylvester, a male, female impersonator, who was famous in Paris, performed at a club named The City. He came up to me at a burger joint and said, "You sure are cute." He came back with a picture of himself and put me on the guest list for his next performance. I attended the performance and had an opportunity to meet him backstage. My experience in North Beach taught me to "Don't start nothing, won't be nothing." That is still my being today. I had a great time working in North Beach, and it will always be very dear to my heart. I still visit the area with nothing but tears of joy.

During the week, I continued to work in the office product business and on weekends in North Beach. The office products work was not easy, cold-calling, mailers, and knocking on business doors. I had a quota to fill and was always behind. I was working on a project to sell sixteen wet copiers. I was working with engineers who needed a wet copier to develop a facsimile machine. I was beginning to experience a lot of pressure from my manager, and I will never forget his name (TD). I was married during this time. He pressured me by even throwing my wife and son into my performance. He wanted to fire me. I then talked to the branch manager who was located in Emeryville near Oakland. I told him about my manager wanting to fire me. I explained my deal for sixteen copiers. He then transferred me to the Emeryville office, but I kept my territory in Silicon Valley. Well, lo and behold, I sold sixteen copiers in December (they bought them in December for tax purposes). With those sales, I became the salesman of the month and also the salesman of the quarter. The spirit was with me then! Apple computer was interested in me working for them. I thought it was funny, them asking me. They had recently come out of their garage in production.

I continued to work in the office products industry until 1980. Around 1977, trouble was rising between my wife and me, and we had a child. Several years later, she divorced me and took my son away from me. I was so broken. Prior to our divorce, I left the area to visit my grandparents in Bastrop, Texas, and I worked in Houston. My grandparents didn't know what had happened between my wife and me. So I explained. My grandfather then said, "If you were two banners waving in the air, neither one would outweigh the other."

I did not understand what was meant by banners. My cousin who was raised by my grandparents explained, "The banners, that's a flag you fool." I lived in Texas for about three months and then drove back to California. I soon landed a job with IBM, and my son came to live with me. The spirit again was with me. When troubles occurred, I would pray, praying to a higher power and not knowing who he was, only knowing there was a greater power. During those years, there was some success, but I didn't have the spirit of karma or righteousness. I was like a hamster in a cage, going round and round. I had the spirit, but I regret not knowing him during those years. I lost some of the spirit then. The only active spirit I had left was equality and an end to racial discrimination. This spirit is still in me today.

Keep in mind racial discrimination and inequality played a big part in my life. The biracial couple of Cleophas and Ursula also played a big part in my life. I hated racial discrimination and still do! To hate someone based on the color of their skin or to hate because of nationality or religion, I do not like that! Now, it's gender, and I don't like hatred there either. Using a color to describe a person, like black or white, is not cool either. In the words of the late Micheal Jackson, "I don't want to live my life, being a color." I am an African American, ethnically; nationally, I'm American. If a person wants to discuss their ethnicity with me, fine. If they were born in America, they are American to me. Keep in mind, this country was invaded. The slaves they brought in did not know they would become Americans, and here comes Obama!

I got married on October 30, 1971, to a beautiful girl. She was the homecoming queen of her college. In Los Gatos, California, 1973, she bore me a beautiful son. From that day until the present, my prayer for him and us is, "Dear God, bless Andre. Help me to help him, and help him to help me." Unfortunately, our marriage did not last, and we divorced several years later. As I look back, we married for the wrong reasons. A year or two later, our son came to live with me in Los Gatos, California, where he was born. Unfortunately, my drug involvement was escalating. I was arrested for cocaine possession and went to jail. That day, my son had no way to get home from school. His mom was able to care for him until I got out of jail. My mom bailed me out this one and only time. I promised her to never touch cocaine again—how wrong I was.

My major concern was my son. What's up with his future? Will he not want to live with me anymore? It had always been my son's choice of who he wanted to live with, me or his mom; there was no back and forth. Even after the arrest, he wanted to stay with me. I completed my thirty-day sentencing. I then moved to San Francisco. My son spent summers with his mom in Los Angeles, but in school months, he was with me. Education was my number one importance with him, and a 3.0 was required every report card, period. During MLK Day, I would lecture on King. The San Francisco Board of Education heard about this and offered me a job for one year to lecture to junior high students. It all worked out, and he lived with me all throughout high school.

Being a single parent and male was very rewarding. When going to a saloon, my son could not go into the bar. He had to wait in the lounge area with coloring or a book. When I checked up on him,

I saw all these girls surrounding him. They would ask, "Oh, is this your son? He's so cute." I'm thinking I should do this more often, and it was fun. My main objectives with him were education and independence; both were selfish on my part because it would transfer some of my responsibilities to him. For example, he had to clean his own room. Then I talked to him about getting a job. He got his first job working with me at Custom Car Alarms. He then went out and got his own job. As a younger child, he had a problem with eating too much candy. I would sometimes clean his room and find loads of candy wrappers. For many years, I barred him from his Halloween candy, only to find myself eating it. Soon after, he came home. "Hey, Dad, I got a job."

I said, "Where?"

He answered, "The Fudge Factory."

Well, "Shit," was what I could say.

After years of monitoring his candy habit, well, he got a job. He stayed on that job long enough and taught me how to melt chocolate. Today, I can do chocolate strawberries in minutes time, thanks to him.

My son, while attending Lowell High School in San Francisco with a 3.0, only missed that grade point once during his tenure. He wanted to participate in the Junior Reserve Officer Training Corps (ROTC). I was disappointed because I wanted him to play sports. I asked my brother-in-law about it. He advised me to support him. So I did. When I first attended his rifle competition, I cried for joy! It was seeing my son so professional, so focused, comfortable, and enjoying himself. I could not help but cry.

My son was promoted to colonel in the ROTC, which was the top-ranking student officer in charge. After graduating from Lowell, he decided to enlist in the Marine Corps. Again, I was against it because I had worked hard to get him admitted into Cal Berkeley. He chose the Marines. His mom and I had to sign the papers for him to enlist because he was only seventeen.

He had skipped first grade because they promoted him to second grade. The reason was, his mom and I had him in preschool at age three and a half. So when he attended kindergarten, he knew it all and then wanted to play, which was disruptive. So at four and a half or five, he was in the second grade.

A girlfriend and I went to Camp Pendleton to see him graduate from boot camp. He carried the honor flag as a lance corporal. I was very proud and also felt guilty. I was a functioning drug addict, yet I kept it on the down low. Also, that was the last time this girlfriend and I were together. I loved her, but what did I know about love? I was a drug addict. I wish her well, and whenever using the word, truly, I think of her. The next time I saw my son was at 29 Palms. My son is now on his way to a career in the military. He served four years of active duty and four years of inactive duty. During his military career, he attended the school of linguistics at the Presidio in Monterey, California. When he graduated and was a guest speaker, I didn't make it to the graduation because of drugs. I still regret that to this today.

While in my drug addiction, I was not a thief. All the time living with my mom, I never stole anything. Except, I would dig in the seat of her car, parked in the garage, looking for change. My mom had a neighbor, an elderly woman, who would loan me twenty at a time. I loved that lady; she saw me grow up. She kept her house a mess. I would say to her, "Can't you do something about cleaning up this mess?"

She would always say, "Baby, if you don't like my peaches, stay from up under my tree."

I loved that lady. She was dancing at my dad's memorial. I said to her, "Hey, you better sit down and get some rest. You're no spring chicken."

She came back quickly with a response. "Yeah, but I can still make the roosters cock-a-doodle-do."

May she forever rest in peace. Friends tried to borrow money from her, but she would never loan. Why me? She knew something about me that I didn't know. That was that I had spirit.

I was born into the spirit never knowing righteousness. My upbringing taught me not to lie or steal, but karma was never taught.

I learned karma as an adult (it's never too late). A very close church friend—we attended church together since birth—taught me about stealing. I was always given money to give to the church. That person showed me how not to give. Instead, I placed the money in my pocket. I was always given a quarter for church. I thought, *Geez, I can buy five candy bars for a quarter, great.* One Sunday, I was taught by this same person how to skip church. So we went to the gym that day and played basketball, and not only did we skip church, but he stole the basketball. That's where I drew the line. I asked, "Why did we have to steal the ball?"

He just said, "Shut up, boy."

Years have gone by, and he and I are now adults and still friends.

I moved back to San Francisco in 1986 after living in Los Gatos. I worked at that time for a car alarm business with a very high-cost markup. As a salesperson, I was able to discount the price, remarkably sometimes a thousand dollars. During that period, a portion of our clientele were people involved in illegal gain, selling cocaine. I personally knew some of the dealers and would discount the price in exchange for drugs. When receiving the drugs, I would immediately share them. One day, after work, my church-skipping friend and I went over to his house and shared the drugs. Oh, we got high and higher. I openly left the drugs on the table and noticed him stealing the cocaine. I also noticed him recording our conversations and playing mind games. He then kicked me out of the house. I would not leave until he returned my drugs. He then went and got a gun, showed it to me, and kicked me out. We later talked about it, apologizing to each other. I never again did drugs with him at his house. We still remain friends.

I once installed an alarm and entertainment system for Robin Williams. It was an awesome experience. I was in Wales in 2014 when I heard he died. I left the alarm business and took the advice of a girlfriend. She encouraged me to enroll in a basic cooking school, a six-month program. I graduated and became a professional cook. I still cook today. I truly enjoy cooking.

What about my friends? In the early seventies, working for IBM, I met several dear friends. Three of them became close friends. Today, only two of them and I stay in close relations; we were sales representatives. We hit it off real good. As of this date, I have never had an argument with one of these friends. When we first met, he was married with two children. I did not know he was having problems at home. He and his wife were separating. I had a two-bedroom apartment, one for my son, but he was away during the summer visiting his mom. My friend lived with me during that summer. He was impressed with the fact that I didn't charge any rent. I did not want a permanent roommate. I wanted to help. He stayed with me for three months, and then he got a two-bedroom apartment. One bedroom was for his girls when visiting on the weekends. From day one of our relationship, he confessed God to me.

During his and his wife's separation, she became a member of the People's Temple with Pastor Jim Jones. Jim Jones was an American religious cult leader. He was the founder of Jonestown in Guyana, South America. He led more than 900 people to their deaths. Ron's wife was in a membership program but canceled the follow-up. Soon after, he and his wife got back together. They adopted two children and eventually took custody of two grandchildren. They also continue to pray for me. We stayed out of touch until 1992.

In 1992, I had a very tragic accident in Austin, Texas. I was there working as a cook and oyster shucker. While riding my bike and buying drugs, a drunk driver came along and hit me. I was thrown forty feet in the air. I was in a coma for seven days and had a compound fracture in my tibia and a compound fracture in my humerus, all because of drugs. Before I went out to buy drugs, I prayed to God for a change. Keep in mind, I really didn't know God at the time but believed in a higher power. God sure brought about a change in me. When I came out of coma for a brief moment, I could only give my mother's phone number because I had no ID on me. I then went back under, and when I came out, my mom was at the foot of my bed. The spirit was with me, again.

I lay in the hospital bed, recovering from the coma and the fractures and thinking about my life, *Now, what am I going to do with my life, what, what?* I had some talent in cooking, but not enough. What am I going to do with my life? The first thing I wanted was peace of mind. I had my mom and her sister removed from the room because they were making too much noise. My mom went through a lot wanting to save my life. I needed peace, to think about my life. My first thought: *Did the suspect have any insurance?* He did, but only one hundred grand, and that barely covered my hospital bill; then come the lawyer, bullshit. He gets one-third, which, after the hospital bill, leaves me with less than $30,000.00. I could have sued the driver for more, by putting a lien on his house, but didn't. I felt we both made an error, and I needed to forgive us both. I was pleased with the settlement and moved on, back to San Francisco to rehabilitate. Now, what about my dreams?

I explained to my good friend from IBM about the accident and how God saved me. He was very pleased to hear that, but I still did not know God. Let me explain that statement, again with better meaning. I knew of a higher power, but my faith was very little, and I didn't know him. I knew my friend continued to pray for me. I love that boy! He and his wife's prayers (along with others) are what helped me become the person I am today. I know God is pleased, but there are lots more work ahead. I am not holy yet but would like to be someday. My buddy from IBM is the best friend I have ever had. He will be mentioned again.

During physical rehabilitation in San Francisco, I had a large stash of marijuana. I learned to mix it with cocaine like a speedball. Marijuana and cocaine combined are very addictive. John Belushi died after injecting a speedball using heroin and cocaine. Now, I am a cook with all of these injuries, no job, no home, and no money. Being at my mother's house was thankfully appreciated, but it was not my home. Mama taught me to provide my own home.

When in 1978, separated from my wife and left for Texas, I stopped by to visit my dad in North Beach. He wanted me to stay.

He said to me with tears in his eyes, "Don't leave, stay. I'll pay for you to visit Disneyland or something."

I said, "No, no, no," and drove off, noticing in the mirror he was crying. That was a very sad moment for me to see my dad cry. That was long ago, and I have tried to live in Texas several times; socially, it sucks, compared to San Francisco. I took a good look at it in 1992, and it still sucked socially, but the women were off the hook. There were lots of girls wanting the experience of an African American male. My time in Texas was short due to the bike accident. Once back in San Francisco, rehabilitation was now my main goal. I had to get back to normality.

After, a year of rehabilitation. I was almost back to normal, ready for work as a cook. I went back to the Hyatt Regency in San Francisco hoping to get back to work, but they had closed the Market Place, which was one of their well-known restaurants. Since I was union, the executive chef did not like me. He had tried earlier before my accident to fire me. He wrongly accused me of being a thief, and he was upset because I had filed a grievance in order to get the job. I also was awarded $5,000.00. Strangely, when my accident occurred in Texas, he had flowers delivered. Trying to get back to the Hyatt was impossible. Since the Market Place was closed, and being the last cook hired, I was bumped out of the way by cooks with more seniority. I decided to work out of the union hall as an extra. I worked all various union houses in San Francisco. Keep in mind, I'm still a drug addict.

During 1992, I worked for all the union houses in San Francisco, the Sheraton Palace, St. Francis, Fairmont, Marriott Fisherman's wharf, The Grand Hyatt, and, at times, the Hyatt Regency. I liked it better because working my own schedule was great and I learned lots from different chefs; it was awesome. Once, I worked thirty-two hours straight, four eight-hour shifts, doing it on drugs. The dispatcher at the union hall was great! I worked out of the hall for several years, making more than twenty-five thousand a year. The spirit was with and in me then. I was thankful to God, but still did not know him or the Holy Spirit or Jesus. I was a drug addict! I took a job from dispatch in Klamath Falls, Oregon, working at a convention for a company called Cell Tech. That is when I became vegetarian and met a good friend, Alex. We are still good friends today.

In early 2000, I quickly went to work for a neighbor in San Francisco. She owned a highland desertlike home in a very rural area outside of Benson, Arizona, and knew of a neighbor needing a chef for a guest ranch. I applied for the job. I went down and worked for the owner, but it did not work out, so I left. Not wanting to go back to San Francisco, I stayed and lived in my San Francisco neighbor's guesthouse. I quickly learned how to drive to Tucson and buy drugs, near the university. I had income from unemployment transferred to the post office in Dragoon, Arizona. It is where I lived. I then began to look for work elsewhere. I landed a job at Benson Country Club. I was strictly vegetarian at this time, eating no fish. The chef gave me a test to cook a veggie soup, and it sucked. I didn't have experience in cooking soups, although I stayed for a week, before getting fired. I had compared myself to this coworker who was a cowgirl. I watched her cook a clam chowder using fusion as a method, which was another lesson for me. I took this method to heart and went back to San Francisco. Fusion or fuse is creating a combustible matter where the flavors mix together but never burn. This method of cooking is what separates the professionals from the nonprofessional, remember to fuse. After leaving the country club, I quickly went back to San Francisco. Hold on, hold for a minute, let me rap.

> I had this dream growing up with me.
> Thinking about life and how it should be
> I thought, things had changed in 2008.
> Obama the first, but then they began to hate.
> How wrong we were, the dream had not come true
> When in the next election Donald Trump came
> through.
>
> I have a dream today.

One nation under God is the American way
So why am I pleading for righteousness today
Forget about slavery and such
Let's work on unity, oh so much.

I don't want to talk about the sons of former slave
owners
Or the sons of former slaves.
If you understand the discrimination of color
Then you are my Brother
One nation under God indivisible
And inseparable, biblical.

My Niggas I have a dream today!

I have a dream today! Well, that's my first version of rap, and I will continue later.

Although I miss the Hyatt, I learned a lot from being a union extra. While working at the Hyatt, I volunteered to write in the employee newsletter under the name Gibby's Gab. I was still doing drugs at the time. I maintained my priorities, but the drugs were still a deterrent. Writing the newsletter allowed me interaction with management. The chef I believed was told hands off me. When working at the Moscone Center during a Macworld convention, I saw and served several of my IBM buddies, who now worked for Apple. I had the opportunity to work for Apple also. During that time, they had just come out of a garage. I would not leave IBM for them, plus I truly wanted out of the business (the spirit was with me). I left the office product business in Silicon Valley. I took on the business of steam cleaning restaurant flues, a dirty business, but I loved it. I steam-cleaned restaurant flues, cooking equipment, and floors. When moving to San Francisco, I took the business with me. I then went to work for the car alarm and cellular phone business. I was not very happy with working the business and continued drug involvement.

When an ex-girlfriend and I got back together, she moved up to San Francisco and got us an apartment on 17th and Clement St. I had gotten out of the steam cleaning business after eight years. I now was in a six-month program on basic cooking, from bread to mother sauces, sanitation, and proper use of utensils. I was about to become a cook. The instructor was a South African German who was a racist. I went to the school's director with my complaints. Now that I look back, this is where the blacklisting began.

He was a master chef from CIA (Culinary Institute of America) and part of the chefs federation. The chef at the Hyatt was the San Francisco chapter president. I'm sure this is why I had to file a grievance to get a job there. The spirit was with me then. I worked at the Hyatt for more than three years before being laid off. Then I took the job in Arizona and returned to the union hall. I thank God for the hall. This present day, I now collect a retirement pension from the union. An offer from a relative came to me to work in Seattle. I worked in Texas, Arizona, Oregon, and now Seattle.

I am now considering Seattle. Moving there may be great, but leaving behind my life in San Francisco, um, I'm not sure. I'm leaving all that I accomplished, education and experience, behind. I had to stop and think about it all. I'm remembering people and events. I worked at the Fairmont Hotel in pantry. I prepared salmon for Mikhail Gorbachev. I designed a concession and wrote a multicultural menu for Candlestick Park; it was the first of its kind. It was an outdoor concession at gate A, with foods from almost every culture in San Francisco. I worked with Gavin Newsom when he was campaigning for his first-time mayorship. His campaign manager, Jim Ross, hired me to cater an event for him. Although I worked as a campaign volunteer in my neighborhood, I also cooked in my hood and was well-known for good food. I would have to give all of this up and also drugs. The drugs were what I was running from, little did I know about Seattle.

I lived with and worked for a relative in Seattle, but it didn't work, and I moved out. I went to work as a chef in Tukwila for a Bosnian restaurant. I learned how to cook Bosnian food, and it was a great experience. I got an apartment, shared with a Bosnian room-mate, and we became good friends. When coming to Seattle, my drug addiction was on hold for about two months, and it quickly started up again. I found a source down the street in a district called Capitol Hill. I was back in the drug business. My Bosnian friends were also smoking crack, straight up. Remember, I was mixing it with marijuana, and they were smoking it straight, although we were all addicted. I found an activity that helped me during the time of addiction, and it was dancing. When getting high with them, I would dance. These neighbor girls would help me with coordinations. They would say, "Ayres, move your hips more." I loved that!

We had a friend who never smoked crack before and who decided to try it. Within two months, he sold his car for crack, charged up all his credit cards, and was evicted from his apartment, and he moved back to Bosnia. I learned a lot about their culture and the breakup of Yugoslavia; it was sad. It was never the same after their long-time president, Tito, died.

I was working for a temporary agency, not as a cook, but I took any labor-type work in order to pay my rent. I soon found out our lease on the apartment was up. My roommate was behind on the rental payments, which I did not know. So they would not renew our lease. I did not want to be without a home, so I checked into a motel with monthly accommodations. After one night of drugging, I went out to buy more drugs and was attacked. I suffered a dislocated disc and shoulder and was taken to a hospital. I now could not work. For the first time, I was without a home, homeless. The hospital discharged me and set me up in a shelter, DESC. I now had a home, but not permanent. I was able to file a complaint to the crime victims department and received $2,000.00. Once able to work, I bought a car and lived out of it.

I worked for the temp agency and made a good weekly salary. I saved up enough money for the first and last month's rent, plus deposit. Landlords have a policy to complete an application along with an application fee. If you were approved for an apartment, then the fee would be applied. If not approved, then they kept the fee.

Well, it didn't take a rocket scientist to figure out; this was not going to work. That's when I took the money, saved and bought a car, and lived out of it. I had wheels now and work, but no home; the car was my home. I moved from out of the Tukwila area into Seattle. I worked a deal with a towing company to park inside their tow yard and help with security. Between jobs, I picked up another job, driving for drug dealers.

A temporary cook's position was available for an in-house hospitality catering company. This was the same company I worked during the Macworld conventions. I was hired on schedule. They were nominated one year as one of the top 100 companies to work for in Seattle. I was an all-around cook, which meant I could work any and all stations. I worked there for two years. A cook during the day and drug chauffeur at night—it did not last long. Oh, I forgot to mention, while living in Tukwila, I worked for Starbucks at the SeaTac airport and learned a lot. I was approved to work at the airport, me, a drug addict. The spirit was with me then. I did not know that, from Starbucks back to the temp. agency.

I have now cooked professionally in Arizona and Texas. I learned lots in Texas, how to smoke brisket and fry fish. I went all the way to Texas to learn how fish is fried. The spirit was with me then, thank God. New Mexico is where I learned Tex-Mex. In Albuquerque, at the restaurant Frontiers, I studied Tex-Mex fusion. Throughout this journey of my life, the spirit was always in me, surrounded me, but I did not know this. Ask yourself: How could I survive? All those injuries, and it's not over for me. Now I'm back in San Francisco. I arranged a birthday party for my aunt's eightieth, at Third Baptist in San Francisco, a very well-known church. The church membership is more than one hundred years old, and I became a member.

I went back to the union dispatch office for work, but applying for a permanent job that was union was impossible. This was because the chef at the Hyatt Regency put the word out on me. Once while working at the Regency, he was drunk in his office. He came out and yelled at me and called me a thief. I forgave that and did not file a grievance. He later apologized.

I learned a lot from being a union extra and volunteered to write in the employee newsletter, under the name Gibby's Gab. I was still doing drugs at the time. I maintained my priorities, but the drugs was still a deterrent. This allowed me interaction with management and it was put to the chef, hands off me. I worked the Moscone Center. During a Macworld convention, I saw and served several of my IBM buddies, who now worked for Apple. I had the opportunity to work for them too, but during that time, they had just came out of a garage. I would not leave IBM for them, plus I truly wanted out of the business (the spirit was with me). I left the office product business.

Since being a kid, I have always wanted to improve things, but that did not include me. Self-improvement is needed if I want to help this world become a better place. I am still working on helping to improve myself.

It's now the year 2013, and I'm still living in my apartment. I'm still working polishing shoes and doing some minor repairs. I'm still a drug addict. I live in a neighborhood filled with hospitality food service and bars, lots. Before getting my apartment, while I was living at the Roy Street shelter, I worked for the catering company. I would get off work and walk through the neighborhood where I am now living. I would say to myself, "This seems like a fun neighborhood." The neighborhood is called Belltown. During my residency here, Belltown was the sixth fastest-growing district in the nation. How is it that I live here? The community education and experience was and is off the hook. There is the Port, Starbucks, Google, Cisco, Microsoft, and Amazon, all in one district. It would be foolish for a person living in Belltown not to take advantage, so I did, even still as a drug addict.

I would often visit a restaurant a few doors from my home. I once got drunk trying to get up from the chair. A staff person asked, "Ayres, are you okay?"

I said, "Trying to get home."

She asked, "Where do you live?"

I said, "Across the street."

Later that year, I landed a job at that restaurant, a dream job, a job I had prayed for. I am now working for the best employer ever. I've worked for some very reputable companies, IBM, 3M, and Royal typewriter, to name a few. Though this employer is the best, only my dad was better. My connection with my boss is one to treasure. My relationship with him and the chef is built into honesty, indulgence, reliability, and trust. With this work criteria, I have excelled as a respected coworker. This feeling was like my successful days working in Silicon Valley. I never ever want to lose this feeling of respect.

I could never have achieved this being a drug addict. Truly, without integrity, the respect could never be. Can a drug addict have rectitude? If not, how could they achieve true respect? Addiction doesn't stop and think about selfishness or harm reduction. It's like that hamster in a cage going round and round, not getting anywhere. Then in comes karma. You must reap what you sow. I could have only achieved this being off of cocaine.

Smoking marijuana itself hasn't been harmful to me; currently, it does not interfere with my righteousness. In my case, marijuana is one of the things that empowers me spiritually. Spiritual righteousness is how I want to live my life until I die! I want to truly love everyone. As I've said before, I don't have to like you, but I must learn to love you. I don't think I will ever be able to love everyone. What is most important is, I'm aware of this lack of love. I hope to spend the rest of my life working on it.

In 2019, after several years of cocaine sobriety, I decided to take two months in Wales, UK. I wanted to visit my son and watch my grandchildren grow. I also began writing this book. My gut feeling this time around is feeling good about one's self and secure about me. I carry with me always a time for improvement in righteousness. Case in point: once in San Francisco, while riding Bart to the airport, I spilled something on the floor. Immediately, wanting to clean it up, I wiped it up with a pair of clean underwear that I had in my bag, thinking I would not want this mess in my home or workplace, what goes around comes around. My connection with humanity will continue to grow spiritually and righteously. Righteousness and karma are two of the three reasons for my success. So what's the third? Huh? I'll get to that later.

My visit to Wales was one of the best in my life. I found Wales to be more socially sophisticated. We all lack righteousness. Do you know anyone perfect? We all, as a world, can improve righteously. If that righteousness can be worldly unified, oh what a wonderful idea. If humanity had respect toward each one's worship and threw in some love, this would be a better world to live in.

What more did I learn in Wales? I was there for two months, and 50 percent of my time was spent writing. Hold up a minute! I have something to say. I have to talk about how the spirit was with me. Well, humanity, that spirit to me is better known as God Jehovah, my third reason for my success. I am a strong believer and getting stronger every day. I have been born-again since 1992. I did not receive my firm belief until 2017, and that was when I could call him out by name. When I stopped smoking crack, then righteousness came into play. So when visiting Wales, I saw a whole new world.

America is now the Old World to me with its racism and all. We are now in the year 2024, and racial profiling still exists. Recently, I was walking across the street from my home where there are lots of construction these days. I noticed a gentleman about to park. I walked over to him as he was backing in, and he quickly rolled up his window and continued to park. I stood there patiently and said, "Hey, be careful parking here. You're blocking that construction tractor."

He then looked and said, "Thank you." I wondered why he had to roll up his window.

Sure, racial profiling and prejudice exist throughout the world. It involves color, religious beliefs, economics, work environment, athletics, and on and on. An individual sometimes finds prejudice to be easier than understanding. Why not no judgment at all? The territory in Wales where my son lives is Lammas Ecovillage, Tir y gafel, Glandwr. The living there is the best I have ever seen. I lived there in 2019 for two months. Not once did I ever feel any racial prejudice or profiling, not once, and they say that this is the Old World? The community is the best I have ever visited. It was like being separated from the rest of the world and not being alone. With friends and family, it was easy living but hard to leave. It was like living in a bubble of protection from the prejudices of America. Speaking of America, which is socially old, I can't think of any territory in the USA with no racial prejudice, unless it is a cult.

In Wales, I enjoyed Tir y gafel, a small community with Lammas meaning (Lammas UK online). The Lammas Ecovillage is essentially a new-built settlement based on the principles of sustainability, biodiversity, and environmentally conscious living. A part of me did not want to leave. I want to keep close to my family in America, so Wales would have to wait.

What more did I learn in Wales? The number one bit of knowledge is that my grandchildren are not experiencing racial discrimination. A good portion of their peers want to be more like them. Thinking about my childhood growing up, I had a very long relationship over ten years with a woman of a different race. Her mom invited me to a Thanksgiving dinner one year. Her father could not sit at the dinner table with me because of my race. This to me was horrible, and I felt no ill feeling toward him. I was living with his daughter. In Wales, my grandchildren will not have to experience this growing up. Those who hate racially need to ask themselves, "What is that hate doing for me?" In my opinion, racial hate is self-motivated. Most of America doesn't endorse it anymore. Those who don't believe in racial hate need to stand up against it. Stand up against it? I will write more on this subject later. It's all about Wales now!

Lammas is a lifestyle that does not endorse hate of any kind, not racial, not religious, nor economical. Lammas is truly the opposite of hate; it's a dream. Yet there are some folks within that community that can be argumentative, although I never felt anything racial. There are disagreements within the community. Not all members believe in God, but they may practice God's righteousness. And everyone I met was spiritual. They all feel loved and know what it means to be loved. Then why in their community meetings do they argue? Sometimes, I think their spirit is left at the wayside, and they forget about love. Those in the community who are not God believers sometimes find love abandoned. We are born into love. Love is in each and every one of us. What do we love most? Most believers in God may say God and then people. Whether you are a believer or not, place righteousness as a priority, and love will follow.

The Tir y gafel community, of which Lammas is a part, is located on the West Coast of Wales. The town Cardigan is on one end, and the town Narberth is on the other end with Tir y gafel in the middle. All of these towns are on the coast of the Irish Sea. Narberth is the town I would visit the most. All of my shopping, drinking, and hair cutting were in Narberth. A very small yet friendly town, the pizza and coffee were awesome. I ate lots of pizza in Narberth, along with my grandkids and son. My experience in Narberth will last a lifetime.

We would drive into Narberth to get to the Irish Sea. I bought a wet suit to better enable me to swim in the sea. I used it, but the water was still cold. I could not muster up enough energy to keep warm. I would just play in the water with my feet. After all the struggles of life with a drug addiction, I was able to experience the good. It was a life not looking for that next smoke of crack, not even thinking about it. The experience in Wales and being with my grandchildren and son were so overwhelming. My first visit to Wales was in 2014. I was also drug-free. That's when I realized that I never wanted to go back to that drug lifestyle again. Sure, I had loved ones in my life during my addiction. I was born into that—siblings, Mama, and Daddy were the norm. When my grandchildren came into my life, life became a new day, a new beginning and drug-free, free from addiction with monies in my pocket and money to give! Let us not forget about karma. I also was able to experience not being Black. They referred to me as American. I never liked living my life as a color.

I'm very happy my son chose Wales to start a family. They are not experiencing the discrimination and racism that I went through. My grandchildren's peers consider them equals. Sad to say, Wales does have its racism. I'm not going to say who, whom, or what, but they have their racism. The community of Tri y gafel/Lammas is not racially interested and is very friendly. The guesthouse where I lived had a couple of horses and a pony. I once owned a horse, which I trained and broke at eighteen months; I know horses. I would take the pony out for walks. One time, as we were walking, my grandson was on the pony's back. This community has tour visits from people all over the world. Each home is self-sufficient, providing its own power and running water completely off the grid. The tour bus pulled up as my grandson and I were walking with him on the pony's back. A guest ran off the bus to greet us with total excitement, waving her hands and walking toward us, wanting to talk. I shouted out, "Hey, wait a second, I don't live here. I live in Seattle." Wales is truly a dream come true.

The best food I have ever eaten was in Wales. Most families in the community have what they call a polytunnel, like an indoor plant nursery. My son and his family grew everything in the polytunnel. There was an apricot tree, a peach tree, a pear tree, and strawberries, tomatoes, collard greens, spinach, different kinds of herbs, broccoli, and almost every food imaginable, all organic. The community has a grocery store named the Veggie Shack, where you can buy almost every vegetable imaginable, all organic. The community is very rich, very unlike what we may think. Their wealth is in the form of love and be loved. In community meetings, arguments occur when love has been removed.

I know love, 2 Corinthians 13 (laugh out loud) no, loads of love yes. It says in the King James Version:

Though I speak with the tongues of men and of Angels, and have not charity (love) I am become as sounding brass, or a thinking cymbal. In other words, I am then nothing more than the creaking of a rusty gate.

> And though I have the gift of prophecy, and
> understand all mysteries, and all knowledge; and
> though I have all faith, so that I could remove
> mountains, and have not charity, I am nothing

And though I bestow all my goods to feed the poor, and though I give my body to be burned, and have not charity, it profiteth me nothing.
Charity suffereth long, and is kind; charity envieth not; charity vaunted not itself, is not puffed up.
Doth not behave itself unseemly seeketh not her own, is not provoked, thinketh no evil.
Rejoiceth not in iniquity, rejoiceth in truth.
Beareth all things, believeth all things, hopeth all things, endureth all things.
Charity never faileth: but whether there be tongues, they shall cease; whether there knowledge, it shall vanish away.
For we know in part, and we prophesy in part.
But when that which is perfect is come, then that which is in part shall be done away.
When I was child, I spake as a child, I though as a child: but when I became a man, I put away childish things.
For now we see through a glass darkly; but then face to face: now I know in part; but then shall I know even as also am known.
And now abideth faith, hope, charity, these three; but the greatest of these is charity.

This is the true meaning of love from the original King James Version. Now, let me give you the message of that version.
Second Corinthians 13 says:

If I speak with human eloquence and angelic ecstasy but don't love, I'm nothing but the creaking of a rusty gate
If I speak God's Word with power, revealing all his mysteries and making plain as day, and if I

have faith that says to a mountain, "jump", and
it jumps, but I don't love, I'm nothing.
If I give everything I own to the poor and even go
to the stake to be burned as a martyr, but don't
love, I've gotten nowhere. So, no matter what I
say, what I believe, and what I do, I'm bankrupt
without love.
Love never gives up.
Love cares more for others than self.
Love doesn't want what it does have.
Love doesn't strut,
Doesn't have a swell head,
Doesn't force itself on others,
Isn't always first,
Doesn't fly off the handle,
Doesn't keep score of sins of others,
Doesn't revel when others grovel,
Takes pleasure in the flowering of truth,
Puts up with anything,
Trust God always,
Always looks for the best,
Never looks back,
But keeps going to the end.

Love never dies. Inspired speech will be over some day; praying
in tongues will end; understanding will reach its limit. We know only
a portion of truth, and what we say about God is always incomplete.
But when the complete arrives, our incompleteness will be canceled.

We don't yet see things clearly. We're squinting in fog, peering
through a mist. But it won't be long before the weather clears and the
sun shines bright. We'll see all then, see it all clearly as God sees us,
knowing him directly just as he knows us!

But for now, until that completeness, we have three things to
do to lead us toward that consummation: trust steadily in God, hope
unswervingly, and love extravagantly, and the best of the three is love.

Some people do not believe in God or a God. What about what the Bible suggests, love, righteousness, good over evil, and loving thy enemy? With these suggestions taken into one's life, it's a no-lose situation. I believe we awake karma's attention when we practice righteousness.

As karma emerges, it then recognizes your righteousness and practice of these biblical suggestions. You can forget about God if you choose, but please inherit the biblical suggestions. I have learned it feels good to be good, truly good. To follow the law that was given to Moses feels really good to me. I love that feeling! You compare good vs. evil. Is this a fair comparison? Are they opposites? Can you equalize them? I don't think so. Looking back on my success, good is good, and evil is evil. If you truly believe in karma, this surely is true. Karma exists y'all, and so does reaping what you sow. What does *reaping what you sow* mean?

Sowing is to cultivate your growing process after planting, while reap is to gain what you have cultivated. Apply this in life, and cultivate using biblical suggestions. So laugh out loud does not apply here; lots of love does. I have learned to love a person and not like them. I may not like their lifestyle, although love is a must. It's a lifelong process for me, sometimes a battle. Righteousness, which I feel is love-related, can help assure love. Righteousness is morally good. The more righteous you become, the greater your love is. How did this change in my life affect me? I experienced success in almost everything, my jobs, my cooking, my career, and my family relations. The success continues to roll in. When did this all begin? It started when I moved to Seattle in 2005, a drug-infested city at that time. Let me fast-forward to the year 2020.

Greta and David Levinson

Enjoy photos of my Mom and Dad, Son and
Grandchildren,Sisters and high way 101 along the west coast
from Oregon to the Redwoods to San Francisco.

national express
IN THIS TEMPLE
AS IN THE HEARTS OF THE PEOPLE
FOR WHOM HE SAVED THE UNION
THE MEMORY OF ABRAHAM LINCOLN
IS ENSHRINED FOREVER

HOW MUCH HAPPINESS CAN 3 YOUNGSTERS SHOW?

It's 2020, I'm still living in Seattle, and Seattle is still drug-infested. The George Floyd incident has arisen, and the pandemic is here. Black Lives Matter is now the slogan of the day. Racism is on the table again with a vengeance throughout America. President Trump is up for reelection. The worldwide pandemic has everything on hold with the exception of racism; it's alive and kicking.

Hold up, there is something different from the racist protests of the past. More Caucasian protestors are saying, "We are tired of this racist crap." It felt like Obama all over again, after his first presidential win. America's constitution is still not living up to its promise. Trump's reelection campaign, I feel, helped diminish the Black Lives Matter movement. Americans once again lost a chance to be racist-free. I treasure the thought of this country being antiracist, and I always will. The only weapon I have to combat racism is righteousness. Being known and seen as a true practitioner of righteousness is the key to achieve goodness. My educator is the *King James Version Bible*. Then I rely on my self-motivated garden (to reap what I have sown), and the reward sometimes comes in honor. I believe there is more good in this world than evil. When the evil in us sees good, we may think about a change in life. Righteousness and karma are good.

You must remember, I grew up during the hippie movement, working in North Beach, San Francisco. I was young, fourteen to twenty-six years old. Free love, compassion, and marijuana were fashionable then, and I was for the taking. Trying this lifestyle in Seattle now would not fly, and since moving to Seattle, I have learned to love its people. Most of whom I know are good, although Seattleites are more presumptive and assuming than San Franciscans. Still yet I have two cities I'm insanely in love with. I will learn from both cities. I will apply my knowledge and experience in order to help those in need of housing, drug rehabilitation, spirituality, and employment. Now, after more than five years of drug-free sobriety, I truly have the integrity to bring about a positive impact. I can do it with God's help. When I moved to Seattle, I did leave my heart in San Francisco. I have grown accustomed to Seattle, and I'm still learning its culture. I know I can make a positive impact because I know God.

My experiences in North Beach impacted my life forever—the El Matador, featuring Cal Jader; Basin Street West; Mr. D's, later becoming the Keystone; and all the strip clubs, exciting. The Playboy Club had a great dramatic impact on my young adult life. I met a lot of famous entertainers and athletes, to name a few, Reggie Jackson, Willie McCovey, Bill Cosby, and the famous lawyer, Melvin Belli, whom Perry Mason's TV character was based on. These experiences helped build my character; every day working in North Beach was a party. After my work was finished with North Beach, I was stuck with my job, selling office products. It was boring yet rewarding, and my reward was income. I was not happy. I had forgotten my work ethics and work integrity. I became lazy, until I came to Seattle and until I became drug-free. I have a job and career here in Seattle. I never have to work another day in my life because I love what I do! Thinking back, this was the young me until cocaine came into play.

Back in 1980, I decided to leave office product sales. I started a business, steam cleaning restaurant flues. Later, I would steam clean the restaurant's cooking equipment. I provided this service for eight years, but I had no love for it. My biggest reward other than money was education, until cocaine came into play, which was then my biggest enemy. After eight years of this business, I wanted to make a change. A good friend suggested that I attend a basic cooking school and learn how to be a professional cook. To this day, that was the best suggestion ever given to me. I will always feel indebted to that person.

I think there was a connection. Since leaving the Hyatt, I have cooked professionally in many states along the West Coast. My cooking profession ended in Seattle. In others words, I stopped cooking for an employer. I now work for a restaurant in Seattle, not as a cook but as a gofer. I am anything and everything. Responsibilities consist of opening, cleaning, painting, fixing, and assisting. My employer is one smart individual, and I learn so much from him.

My current job is where I first started applying righteousness, loving my coworkers, and practicing integrity in my work. I do my best. This began around the year 2014 after my return from Europe.

I know my son and grandkids had a huge impact on me to change my life for the better and better and better and better. Since being drug-free, I get up every single day loving life, and I'm thankful for it. I thank God every day. I feel this way even when I'm sick or discouraged. How do I achieve this? Through my practice and worship of God, righteousness, and karma. You can achieve the same through karma, but without your faith in God, you will not achieve eternal life, this I know, although eternal life does not interest me as much as here on earth does. I love my coworkers, family, and friends very much, and I love my job.

It's now 2022, and I'm still living in Seattle and loving life. Ah, the memories of my life are very enjoyable yet frightening. Thinking back to 1966 while driving into Austin, Texas, on a family vacation, we were delayed at the entrance of the city due to a sniper on top of a large building. This person succeeded in killing fourteen people. That incident became world news and history that would last for decades. My family and I experienced a terrible act. It had a great impact on my childhood, good vs. evil; choose, but choose wisely. I never thought one person would try to achieve such an act.

I cherish my memories. What's happening now in Seattle in 2022? Where am I going to go from here in 2022? Loving life is just not enough. I want to share this love of life starting with my community. Within my community, there are people without a permanent home, people with drug addiction, and people with low self-esteem who maybe are on medication. I believe the solution to these problems is karma. If you believe in God, karma still applies, the principal of karma. Good intent and good deeds contribute to good karma and happier rebirths, while bad intent and bad deeds contribute to bad karma and bad rebirths. This concept has also been adopted in Western popular culture, in which events that happen after a person's actions may be considered natural (fate) consequences. What about those with mental issues on medication or those who are mentally unstable with no sense of reality? Karma takes good care of them. They are housed with caretakers. Most have the sense of good and bad, mostly causing no harm to themselves, which would be bad.

The mentally ill try mostly to live a good life. Mentally ill people need professional help. It's all our responsibility to help those in need. If in your community there are mentally ill people wandering the streets, you should try and feel their pain.

Thinking about Arizona, before moving to Seattle, I quickly went to work for a neighbor in San Francisco, around the year 2003.

Wait a second. Hold on, hold on. Let me continue to rap.

> Growing up with me, a dream
> Thinking about life and how it should be
> I thought things had changed in 2008
> Obama the first, but then they began to hate.
> How wrong I were, the dream had not come true.
> When the next election Donald Trump came through.
>
> I have a dream today.
> We shall live as one and have fun!
>
> One nation under God is the American way.
> So why am I pleading for righteousness today?
> Forget about slavery and such.
> Let's work on unity, oh so much
>
> I have a dream today.
> We shall live as one and have fun.
>
> America needs to live out the Creed
> A true formula to address its need
> Let's all come together under a National umbrella
> With love, hope, and creed.
>
> I don't want to talk about the sons of former slave owners
> Or the sons of former slaves.

If you understand the discrimination of color.
Then you are my Brother.
One nation under God indivisible.
And inseparable, biblical.

My Nigga's I have a dream today
I have a dream today.
We shall live as one and have fun for ever more
(repeat).

I was invited to Seattle by a relative. I was not looking to visit but to live. A change in lifestyle is what I was looking for in Seattle. I was a drug addict and wanted a change from that addiction.

Mixing crack with marijuana was my choice of addiction; coming from smoking crack, this was not as addictive, expensive, and less troublesome, but still addictive. Smoking crack/pot is a mind-altering substance that was slowly taking away my dreams in life. You get that feeling of euphoria, but what can you do with it is not much because you're stoned. When you're high, yeah, you feel great and, yeah, you can do anything, but eventually, the high wears off. I was in a state of mind where I just did not care. I would have to stop smoking in order to pick back my dreams.

I became tired of this, and it was getting old and at time worthless because I could not get back to my dreams. So I thought Seattle would be a good change to get away from drugs. I did not know that Seattle is very prevalent in crack, heroin, alcohol, and marijuana. I was not ready for this rude awakening.

At this point in my life, cocaine and marijuana usage has been thirty or more years and habitual usage twenty off and on. I realized if I want to live out my dreams, I had to stop. I arrived in Seattle by train, and I could see the view from San Francisco to Seattle. What a beautiful ride, and I'm drug free.

My cousin, whom I was going to work for and live with, was there when I arrived to pick me up. He was great to live with. He was never a problem, with only one exception: he was not very clean in the kitchen. So I took on the responsibility of keeping the kitchen clean.

He is a very successful man, owning several businesses. I worked and lived in his apartment building. I would wake up, eat, and go to work. I learned a lot about painting and drywall work, and it was fun. After working for several months, I learned that drugs, cocaine, pot, and heroin were being sold on the streets, two or three blocks away. I fought it and fought it, not to go there, but three months of sobriety, I thought I could check it out and be safe.

How wrong I was, waiting for a spark that would ignite that desire to smoke crack and pot together. All it took was for me and my cousin not to get along, but any excuse would do. I was back smoking. At first, it was maybe once or twice a week, but within weeks, it increased to almost daily.

I was back into addiction. My cousin kicked me out. Prior to my addiction, I met a person who was interested in my ability to cook. He helped set me up with a cooking job. Prior to my cousin kicking me out, we got into an argument. It was almost a fight because at times, he was very rude. So to get his attention, I tackled him to the ground, and that's when he kicked me out.

I called the police because he just can't kick me out like a dog. I have my rights and no place to go. The police would not let him throw me out in the street. So I said, "Give me one week, and I'll be out." The friend who was interested in my cooking helped me with a job and a place to live.

One night while driving for a dealer, I was stopped by the police. They searched my car and me and found no useable drugs, with the exception of small pieces of crack on the seat. Let me tell you, that car had more cocaine and spermatozoa than the law would allow. They impounded the car and took me to jail. They held me for several hours. Then, a very tall sergeant came to my cell and released me into his office. He said, "We know what you are doing. If we ever catch you again, I'm going to book you."

The next night, I sat in my car and smoked for the last time. I sold my car the next day to a wrecking yard for three hundred dollars and checked into a shelter. I hoped the shelter would help me get into a permanent home. I had never lived in a shelter. The shelter was named First Church. When I was there in 2008, I wrote a poem on paper and hung it on the wall. In contrast to MLK's writing about "I Have a Dream," I wrote "I Had a Dream."

Knowing that not only did African Americans help put Obama in office but Caucasians did more made me very proud of America. Trump became president, how wrong was I? Racism was still on the table, and I wanted rid of it!

Living in the shelter was a very rude awakening. I had never experienced bedbugs. We slept on mattresses on the floor. The mattresses were pushed very close to another in order to make room. I remember being awakened to a fart that was so bad, I immediately got up. There was a volunteer group work within the shelter. I took the bathroom and toilet cleaning, for several reasons mainly because it was the worst. I continued to smoke my drugs, outside of the building, while living in the shelter.

I earned money working the catering company. Since my seniority was very low, I averaged about twenty to thirty hours a week. Most of my money went to drugs, food, and whatever else, but no savings. I was that hamster in a cage, going round and round. Although I wanted out, trying to build enough discipline was tough. I prayed a lot, but prayer without righteousness. I was only spinning. I had to learn how to be righteous.

I learned of a shelter affiliation on Mercer and Roy street. They had case managers assigned to us. My case manager was great, very helpful, and very unconditional, with exception of my drug priorities. He knew I was a drug addict. He also knew of my dreams. I will always miss him. He knew about my smoking crack with marijuana. He several times would ask, "Why don't you try not smoking it for two weeks?"

I did not ever want that. I discussed the possibility of moving to Mercer and Roy, where they had bunk beds, and it was closer to my job.

He said, "I can assign you there."

I asked, "Will I lose you as a case manager?"

He said, "Yes, but I will always be around as a friend."

Well, that was good enough for me. So I moved to the other shelter. I was moving closer toward independence, and it felt great! The spirit was with me!

The bunk beds were comfortable, no more bedbugs and better food. Oh, they fed us, two meals a day, better food than the other shelter. I slept on the top bunk, and the person below, his birthday and mine were on the same day, April 6.

Once, a staff member saw me smoking a rolled item, but they passed it off, not knowing it was marijuana mixed with crack. One evening, a group of people came in from an organization called Reach. They offered a program for housing, if you could prove you had a job of at least thirty hours a week. With my current job, I did not qualify.

While working at the catering company, I also shined shoes on a sidewalk in front of a well-known bar in the Pioneer Square of Seattle. I was paid by donations. I made good money and sometimes turned money away. Some people would give too much, like $40.00. No, I could not accept that. So in order for me to meet the criteria for an apartment with Reach, I began a full-time business with polishing shoes. I got a location at the third tallest building in Seattle. Later on, I met the criteria and got an apartment.

I quit my job with the catering company. I told the sous-chef, "I'd rather shine shoes than work for you." I had a business, and I was looking for an apartment. Hey, like the TV show *The Jeffersons*, "Were moving on up." The spirit was with me, and I'm *still* a drug addict. I enjoyed polishing shoes. The results from shoe maintenance was very rewarding to me and very gratifying. This business, like many of my other endeavors, was to improve the service at less cost. I worked on my character and communications in order to bring festivity into the business. I named myself Woody because of my faux hawk haircut.

A good friend reminded me there is another description of Woody. I said, "Oh, that's right, but I'll keep the name." I worked this business for two and a half years, met some good friends, and learned a lot about business in Seattle, but I was *still* a drug addict, unfortunately.

On my sixtieth birthday, I gave a big party. Most of my shoe maintenance clients attended, and it was a very successful. One client and a good friend brought several of his women coworkers, which always helps make a good party. Yes, I made money, but a large portion went toward sex, drugs, and rock and roll, but I continued and wanted to improve my formula for my success.

To my family and friends, these are words to live by: 2 Corinthians 5:16–20, from https://www.biblegateway.com. I prefer reading the King James Version because it allows a greater understanding for me. It says:

> Because of this decision we don't evaluate people by what they have or how they look. We looked at the Messiah that way once and got it all wrong, as you know. We certainly don't look at him that way anymore. Now we look inside, and what we see is that anyone united with the Messiah gets a fresh start, is created anew. The old life is gone; a new life emerges! Look at it! All this comes from the God who settled the relationship between us and him, and then called us to settle our relationships with each other. God put the world square with himself through the Messiah, giving the world a fresh start by offering forgiveness of sins. God has given us the task of telling everyone what he is doing. We're Christ's representatives. God uses us to persuade men and women to drop their differences and enter into God's work of making things right between them. We're speaking for Christ himself now: Become friends with God he's already friends with you.

Please allow me to focus on this scripture, as I want to wear it out!

Let's say, for example, you don't believe in a God or any supernatural being, okay. Where does your goodness come from or your badness? Living life, we have two main choices, good or bad. So which do you choose? Keep in mind, I'm writing this book. So let me tell you, growing up and into adulthood, bad was my way of life, lying, cheating, and stealing. This was internally me, but the outside appearance and action were not me. It was evil. This bad in me most of the time was never acted out, but it was in my heart. Why did I sometimes choose bad over good? Because it was an easy way out!

The truth, which is good, can be hard work than bad. Cheating is bad and unrewarding. When you cheat, you stop the growing and learning process. We all know how important truth is to us. Lying is an easy way out. When you lie, you stop the truth, which then becomes unknowable. Stealing is an unaccomplished act. Remember karma? You gain no reward from stealing and no sense of self-worth. How can you have any feeling of integrity when you steal? Lying, cheating, and stealing—I was again that hamster in a cage going round and round. My drug addiction only magnified this situation. Then I realized, I was my worst enemy. I was more harm to myself than anyone else. This had to stop, and it did, only through the help of Jesus, my teacher! Although I am not without sin, I learned through Jesus not to lie, cheat, or steal. Now he is teaching me how to love. A lot of folks I don't like, but I love them. I am trying to love everyone. It's not easy for me.

Hold the press! Something has come to my attention, regarding my integrity. Not only is this my opinion, but it's a matter of Christian conjecture. I most definitely need to defend myself and share this with the world. I need you, readers, to believe in me.

My prayer day for community, friends, and family is every Friday. I learned this from a church several years ago. If I sometimes miss a Friday for prayer, I will do it on a Saturday. A person came to visit me at home recently, and we discussed a family member of theirs. He wanted me to add the member in prayer. I asked, "Would you like me to add you and the family member to this list?" Later, when he saw my list, oh boy, that person became appalled his name was not on it. I tried to explain why with reasoning, and but I was pushed for time.

The person walked away saying, "Maybe you can explain another day."

When I pray on Fridays, it's a format, a pattern from A to Z. I start with some businesses that I am most familiar with. Where I work is usually last on my list, and I call out every employee by name. Therefore, you are always on that list of prayer, although your family member you want prayer for is not.

I change my prayer list periodically, and when doing so, I did not include your family member. I'm sorry. It's not so important for me to add this person because you are in control of praying for this person. Yes, you and only you control your own destiny, you. This is what I believe and write about, people's control of their own lives.

Yes, readers! Believe me, we all are responsible for our own destiny. I made the mistake of sharing my go-to prayer with someone. All I need to say with a person in need is, "I will keep you in prayer." It's not necessary to talk about or discuss my prayer list. This was a lesson/exercise learned.

My learning of the biblical practice is, "Reaping what you sow," and my knowledge of karma has strengthened integrity in me. I know me now better than ever, no more insecurities about my purpose in this life. I now know my purpose is to help this world become a better place to live, starting with myself as a good person and witness to others. Although I will never be without sin, I know my sinful ways. I try not for them to affect others. I am my worst enemy. Why? Because I don't always follow the rules of karma.

Karma, that's a big word, an important word to understand. I truly believe it's involved in all of our daily lives. How does it affect us daily? What are we doing to help the person without a permanent home? Remember karma, and if they are a nuisance, what are you doing to help their situation (remember what goes around)? In the Bible, there are more than twenty scriptures that talk about helping the needy. What are you doing to help? This problem of people living on the streets will never get resolved until we all get involved. Our politicians should stop talking about it; instead, they should be doing something about it. In the words of Micheal Jackson again, "Take someone by the hand." To me, the person who's unwilling to help is no different than the person who needs help.

My biblical practice has brought me great rewards. Let me name a few: good health, a good home, a dream career (for me), a savings account, vacations, and commuting long distance monthly. I wake up joyous and happy mostly every day. My only problem at times is anxiety. You must remember, we are individuals, and each one of us is different. My problem may not be your problem. If we all come together under that spiritual umbrella of "what goes around comes around," this world would be a better place to live. Case in point, cigarettes are legal, and they bring great pleasure. They can also bring cancer and death, and alcohol consumption can do the same.

Our government allows companies to endorse these products. How could they ever help those in need? Our politicians still use the word *homeless*, those idiots. Remember the term *handicapped*? How derogatory! Every human being in this world has a home. Some may consider a shopping cart with all their belongings their home. I would like to see them (police) take a shopping cart away from them. Sure, people sometimes are down on their luck. People who lack spiritually, with drug addictions and with unconventional housing, can never emerge without good karma. To those people who complain about people without a permanent home, the problem will never be solved until they get involved. I'm on the outside now looking in on the situation. I love you all!

I have said this before, I can love you and not like you. I may not like your lifestyle, but I will do my best to love you. What about the times when you argue with someone? Does it mean you don't love them? At the time of the argument or the thought of arguing, this is not love, in my opinion. It's hard, folks. I had a career situation where a colleague saw that I was being unsanitary in his opinion. And there was nothing unsanitary about what I did. He criticized me in front of others and lashed back. There was no love there. I never liked this person. I always pretended, although I must say I love him. In the future with this individual, I don't have to pretend anymore, just love him. Love makes the world a happy place to be.

Now I'm a believer in God. The Bible talks about God's kingdom! I believe that kingdom can be achieved here on earth, simply by applying karma. God's kingdom is so beautiful, like you would imagine the Garden of Eden; to me, it's poetic, romantic, and peaceful, where all of your dreams and wishes come true here on earth. Simply by applying karma, I'm traveling through life on a natural high! I think back, if only I knew God in my twenties like I know him now, I would be much happier.

Regarding karma, they say that a person consist of desires; as is his desire, so is his will; and as his will, so is his deed; whatever deed he does, that he will reap. This was said by Brihadaranyaka, a seventh-century philosopher, and the Bible says, "You must reap what you sow." Truly, y'all, we are all in control of our own destiny. A person can use the Bible as a tool for learning about good deeds, and the Ten Commandments is a sure way to follow, and if you can learn to love your enemy, boy, you've reached perfection. Good luck! Three other books that are very good to learn about good deeds are the Torah, Qur'an, and books on Hinduism.

No one on this earth is a perfect humanitarian; we all have come very short of perfection; therefore, there are lots of room for growth. Jesus, here on earth, is the only person I learned of who was perfect. Who is perfect? No one is, but the growth process can be rewarding. Take a look at the benefits through karma of being good and the complications of being bad. Which would you choose? Love and karma go hand in hand, and applying these two, you will not lose in life. Let's take a look at karma and the law that was given to Moses.

The law given to Moses are the Ten Commandments. Let's see if I can remember them all. They will not be in order. "Thou shall not put any person above thy God, nor create any graven image of a God." That word *graven*, what does it mean? A graven image is an idol, an object, or image, such as a statue, that is worshipped as the representation of a deity or god. The word *graven* means carved or sculpted. Some form of worship feel wearing a cross in representation of Jesus is sinful. Wearing of the cross is not a graven image but does represent Jesus's death as a believer. Back to the commandments: "Thou shall not steal, keep the sabbath day holy, thou shall not commit murder, thou shall not commit adultery, thou shall not use God's name in vain, thou shall not bear false witness to thy neighbor, thou shall honor thy mother and father, and last, do not covet thy neighbor." These are all good, not bad, and an easy guide toward perfection. Good luck!

When I first learned of the law, I thought it to be easy; it's no way easy. Only Jesus was able to perfect this, the law. The law has helped me achieve all that I have of good. I have reaped what I have sowed. My ultimate reward is now three beautiful grandchildren. As children growing up, they are experiencing much less racism than I did.

My generation of siblings are God-fearing. The person who uses the term *God Damn* is using God's name in vain. What about the person who hates? Yes, I hate evil, and I'm trying to do something about it, by example of karma. This is all very good, but what about the person who thinks evil? Is there any reward for them? I don't think so.

After the law, Jesus came to earth and brought about a new law. That is, to put no other God before our God and to love your neighbor as you love yourself. I want to explore this new covenant of loving yourself. How much do we love ourselves? How about those who end their lives intentionally with suicide? Are they loving themself, um? If I'm not loving myself, how can I love others? A person hooked on using illegal drugs or any addiction is one not loving himself. A person's level of love for themselves may not equal the love needed for someone else. Thank God for believers who are under the guidance of mercy and grace because understanding comes with mercy and grace. Although we must still reap what we sow, what goes around comes around.

I have talked about good karma and gave examples of good karma in my life. What about bad karma? What about children born with birth defects, disabilities, or Down syndrome? I had to research this question. The first was Bahá'u'lláh, an Ottoman educator, who wrote in 1863 of the Bahá'í faith:

> Every human being is created noble and that physical infirmity does not affect the light of the soul. Those who endure and overcome physical challenge possess souls of tremendous capacity and potential. Also, the writings of all faiths affirm the perfection of the creation, so logically the appearance of imperfection is relative, and stems from partial perception. Order emerges when viewing humanity as a single body; thusly we see that some souls, like strong, tall trees, are the cause of the progress of others. Humanity could not understand health without it's deficiency and more importantly, the reality of love, compassion, perseverance, courage, or charity without direct application. A world of imperfection is evidence that a world of perfection exists. Our attraction is thus to the world of perfection and not for this temporal womb world.

All I need to know is what is good or what is bad.

Loving yourself? Jesus has taught me to love myself, truly without a hitch. I really feel love for myself. This is why I want to help others. Love of oneself is the first step, before loving others. You must first love yourself, and then, the world is open to you to help create a better world. You cannot spread love if you don't love yourself. We are meant to harmonize with each other positively and with good intentions; with bad intentions, nothing good will become of it. Love or hate, which would you choose? Jesus is asking you to love yourself. If you don't, how can you love anyone else? I must take care of me with love, before I can love anyone else. If I don't, I'm worthless. Loving one's self with good intentions is unselfish, then you can love your neighbor as you love yourself.

Fate vs. karma? Fate has no spirituality; it's predetermined. We can control karma when making a decision on good or bad. Karma is absolute. I have said before, "What goes around comes around." That's absolute. Which would you believe in, fate or karma?

A letter to the people of America: if you know of the oppression through the years of so-called African Americans in this country, then you are my sisters and brothers. African Americans are the most hated yet most prolific race in the building of this country. On both ends, the oppressor and the victim both discriminate. In most cases, you cannot combat fire with fire. You cannot combat racism with racism; two wrongs do not make it right.

Once African Americans achieved equal rights through the civil rights bill, there was an immediate search for identity. They were first called slaves, then Niggers, Colored, Negro, Black, or African American. They should've stopped at Negro. They should have stood up with pride to say I'm American, and that's it, American. Using myself as an example, I was born at San Francisco General Hospital, and I'm an American. So when the oppressor performs their oppressions, if they are aware they are performing this to another American, it may deter their action.

The beautiful thing about this country is its racial diversity. African Americans, along with our Indigenous people, played a big part in the building of this country. African Americans are simply Americans. It's their nationality, but what about ethnicity? Which comes first, ethnicity or nationality? Well, my ethnicity I share with my family and friends like chitterlings, but history I want to share with the world. African Americans are so persistent to have an African American president, but it wasn't them who put him in office; it was all Americans who voted. You see, karma works, not fate. One of African American's greatest assets was a nonviolent campaign against the oppressor, and this was good Karma.

France's practice of country identification has no skin color identification. The writer of *The Count of Monte Cristo*, Alexandre

Dumas, had a grandmother who was an enslaved Haitian woman. Dumas was a person of African descent, lived in France, and was a Frenchman, not African French. More currently is Yannick Noah born of a Cameroonian father and a French mother. Although he referred to himself as Black, legally, he is a Frenchman. African Americans should've stood up and said, "I'm American. That's what I am, American."

We all have spirit; it's in your soul. Your spirit/soul controls your karma, good or bad. What I love about Jesus is, he teaches us what is good. His teachings are so absolute, you will never lose in life. Jesus is who I choose to follow and learn from. So if you want, just try and practice his teachings, and you will see an immediate positive change in your life. During my drug days, sin did not have dominion over me, personally nor biblically. "For sin shall not have dominion over you: for ye are not under the law, but under grace." This is forgiveness, so move on, and continue to try again. Racist Americans and its victims need to come together in love.

I believe the greatest component to being good is love, and the greatest component to love is learning to love your enemy; that is very, very hard. When you are at war with someone, how can you love them? The Old Testament says, "An eye for an eye."

Jesus says, "To turn the other cheek."

Love is not an easy task. I suggest to try loving your enemy. Take a good look at this practice, practice it, and see the results; give it a try. I wrote earlier about love. I can love you, but not like you. I want the best for you. Both hate and love take a whole lot of energy. One is positive and the other negative. Which do you choose? I choose love with a clear conscience; once applied, it is complete. Hate goes on and on, it seems to never stop. I don't have time in my life for this shit, hate.

Let me take a look at the *Webster* definition of love and hate. *Hate* is to feel intense dislike for something or someone or passionate dislike. *Love* is an intense feeling of deep affection. *Love* is a great interest and pleasure in something or someone. Now, which would you choose, love or hate? They both take an effort, but which one would bring you pleasure? They both would bring pleasure, one of hate and one of love. Which would you choose?

Let's look at *hate*! Does it truly bring you pleasure? After all is said and done with *hate*, does it truly bring you pleasure? What about remorse? Some people feel bad after they hate; is this pleasurable? I don't think so. I learned several years ago how to love, and I wrote about it. Then, I applied it, which was very, very rewarding. Once with a coworker with whom I got into a violent argument, I went home and prayed on our relationship with love in mind. Later that week, he went back to his home country. Love and prayer rid me of him.

One of the greatest requests of God is, learning to love your enemy. Loving my friends will help me in life. How much will hate help you? I know of several people who hate, and then I look at their faces of disappointment, anger, and unhappiness. It's shameful to me. My dad would notice the face of disappointment and say, "Their lip would hang so low, a wagon wheel could roll over it." I know of several people who love. Oh, boy, look at their happy faces. So which would you choose, a happy face or sad face when it comes to hate? Love is what helped me pull out of drug addiction, having poor credit, a negative appearance, inability to travel, and being without a permanent home.

I now spend time thinking of where to travel next. Flying to San Francisco ten times a year is routine. Visiting Wales once a year is routine. Being the single person I am, dates are frequent and fun. Working for a living is incredible. I love what I do, even if it's picking up garbage from the streets; I love it. My mission in life is to better my family and to help this world be a better place. This is my prayer! What steps am I taking to achieve this? First, sharing my experiences to those without spirituality, those drug addicted, and those not having a permanent home. Now, I'm on the outside looking in, and I want to *help* with love. One of the best places to find love is a church, and another is at a bar; it can bring out spiritual meaning, love. Don't you feel good after having a drink? If you have too much, then, you feel bad. Arguments may occur, and you leave unhappy. All good things in moderation should always be in moderation. Too much of a good thing is not healthy.

Too much love is not healthy; think about it when it comes to our children. When parenting, we must sometimes say, "Enough is enough," and then we must get into tough love. Loving our children with the intentions of guiding them through life positively—it is tough! Being a parent was and is my greatest reward. I love my grandchildren, daughter-in-law, and son more each day. My reward is, they love me back, and I like that! Family and friends are so important in our society. You can't get through life without one or the other, and I choose both. Love is very spiritual! True love unconditionally will bring you to greater heights in this world of competition; learn true love.

Competition? How about White Power vs. Black Power? How do you combat the two? They both have power, but which is the greater of the two? It's the one that combats the problem with love. Racism is the problem between the two. If either side would try and solve their problems with love, this would lessen the argument and bring a solution. This is a good example of trying to love your enemy. If hate is set aside, then we can truly see the forest for the trees, toward a good solution. The Black Power movement must know and remember White Power has it all over them. White Power has the power because they are a majority in this country. Case in point, they are more prominent, and it was White Power that enslaved Africans. It was White Power that came up with the Jim Crow law. It is White Power that keeps America in war, oh, and White Power that helped Obama get elected. Obama was won through love, setting our hate aside. Living a life of love is our greatest tool. White Power is here, and Black Power is here to keep it in check (thank God).

This Universe is our greatest confirmation, it works all too well. Remember the television show *The Beverly Hillbillies*. The show aired during the most important time during the Civil Rights movement. The show was very popular in the African American household. It was a very funny show. It highlighted country Hillbillies in Beverly Hills, who were ignorant and uneducated toward city life, and they were Caucasian. This warmed the hearts of many African Americans, knowing we are not the only ones; there are some white folks too. That show helped a lot of African Americans with their self-esteem. Although I didn't see the show through color, I just liked the humor. Karma was on my side. I loved *The Beverly Hillbillies*, despite Granny's love for the confederacy. They were a God-fearing family.

Love vs. hate, which do you choose? Let me define the two. Love is an intense feeling of deep affection, a great interest and pleasure in something. Hate is an intense or passionate dislike for someone or something. Dislike or pleasure, which do you choose? We were not born into this world to hate. We were born into this world to love, a cry at birth and then a smile. The smile is of pleasure, which is love.

And here they say that a person consists of desires, and as his desire, so is his will, and as his will, so is his deed; and whatever deed he does, that he will reap. This is a quote from the Bible. Hate or love plays a big part here. Which do you choose? I try to incorporate love into my deed, my will.

Righteousness should always be considered when performing a deed. Righteousness will improve your productivity, and laziness has no part in productivity. This is how I improved my work performance through righteousness. A person without spirituality, illegal drug addiction, or a permanent home can achieve all three through righteousness. A person without righteousness will never, never achieve success. You must have a sense of righteousness to achieve success. What goes around comes around.

My self-opinion formula for success is, simply, righteousness. Righteous intentions (and I use the Bible to define good) and our deeds will always prove success. Sometimes, the success may not be what you are looking for, but the result is inevitably good, and you can build on that with continued righteousness. Righteousness is not drunk driving, dishonesty, and jail time; these are all bad. The difference between good and righteousness is, being good is being more self-righteous. Righteousness without self spreads the wealth; it's what's good for both you and I and the world. Righteousness entails more work than being just good. Righteousness doesn't lie, and it's unselfish. Hey, it's the same biblical meaning of love! Righteousness is better than good! I achieved my success through righteousness!

Good and righteousness are completely different; righteousness has more meaning and covers more, while being good sometimes is not enough. For me, being good is just being polite. Righteousness requires politeness with additional action, at least prayer follow-up, keeping the situation on hand for some time, and continued prayer. As you are righteous toward another, truly, they will be good to you and maybe even righteous. Righteousness can help eliminate conflict among nations. Righteousness is the key to opening the door of success. All of your dreams can come true through righteousness here on earth. I can image almost like heaven—karma for those and Jesus for us!

What goes around comes around, I believe is very true. That practice has helped me achieve my success. I have always had spirituality not knowing who or what, but somehow, it always got me out of a jam, either out of jail, rehab, accidents, new jobs, or never going hungry, and I always had a roof over my head. I never slept outdoors. I always worked too. While a drug addict, I worked several years for a company. During that time, the company was voted one of the top one hundred companies to work for in Seattle, and I was living out of my car. Even though I was my worst enemy, my goodness helped me achieve these things. Now that I have learned how to be righteous, all of my dreams in life are coming true. Keep in mind, although I try and practice righteousness, I am a Christian and a sinner. I'm not perfect.

So since I sin, how is it that my dreams are coming true? My God, our God, believes in mercy and grace and forgiveness, and so I'm practicing grace with all humanity. I try not to hold any grudges, no hate, or whatsoever. I only want peace with humanity.

I'm learning more about good and righteousness. In the beginning, Genesis 18:19 says:

> For I have known him, in order that he may com-
> mand his children and his household after him,

that they keep the way of the Lord, to do righteousness and justice, that the Lord may bring to
Abraham what He has spoken to him.

This is the way of the Lord! The Ten Commandments and the
New Testament given by Jesus are the way of the Lord! I try my best
to follow them. Moving forward to Mark and looking at the Word
(good), Mark 10:18 says, "So Jesus said to him, 'Why do you call me
good?'" No one is good but One, that is, God. Karma for those and
Jesus for us! I am so blessed and, in the words of karma, so fortunate
to have experienced all that I have. I am able to write about my experiences in order to help others.

Hey, I'm blessed! I apologize to my family for the person I once
was. I feel indebted to them. I'm sorry if I brought about any embar-
rassment, but it was what it was, sorry, my life story!

Righteousness taught me a better way to live, being right with
God. "Thou must reap what you sow," and "What goes around
comes around." "Love your neighbor as you love yourself." And I put
no other God before my God, and karma you must believe. Now,
you are responsible for your own destiny. So what's the problem?
"Shake a leg," "Rock and roll," "Get a move on." Be happy, wealthy,
and glad. Thinking back, I regret not knowing God in my twenties
because all of my dreams would have come true now, although it's
not too late at the age of seventy. Pray for me as I pray for you.

My greatest sin at this moment and time is in the flesh, wasting
the seed of life, and this I must shake, and I will through prayer. I
have lived through all the sin, the hurt, the accidents, the recovery,
and the prayers. One of my greatest experiences was being without
a permanent home, and that humbled me a lot. During that time, I
wondered, *Why, why?* And all I could think about was, *I want to go
home, I want to go home, I want to go home.* So now, with all of the
lessons learned through all the experiences along the way, all the hurt
and pain of being a drug addict, and with the help of God, Jesus, and
the Holy Spirit, I am now home! Here I will be, and here I will stay.

You see, home to me is not just a roof over your head. Home to me is happiness, joy, love, and to be loved; this you must earn.

It feels good to be home!

About the Author

THE VERY FIRST TIME I saw Ayres was through a kitchen window at six o'clock in the morning. He was washing dishes in the nude. I was shocked but secretly delighted. Two weeks later, a friend invited my husband and me to a party. Much to my surprise, it was at Ayres's apartment, and it was his birthday. That evening began a long and close friendship.

We share the same interesting and sometimes gritty neighborhood. On summer days, Ayres puts his table of fellowship through his ground-floor window out onto the sidewalk with a boom box. Everyone is welcome, and many random friendships are formed. Sometimes, Ayres cooks his specialty beef brisket, and the dessert is his famous chocolate-covered strawberries. He is always there to share.

He is interested in our community and frequently contributes to our Belltown Community Council meetings. He can always be counted on to help. During the holidays, he has been known to distribute cash to those in need on the street.

I value Ayres as a close friend. He has added so much to our community and also to my life with his friendship.

—Greta Levinson